DISCARD

FOOD AND MEDICINE FROM THE SEA

Ninety-two nutritional elements have been found in the plants that grow in the sea and the creatures who live in it. As our land is increasingly depleted of nutrients, so do our crops supply less sustenance for good health. But the sea around us has become a vital source of food and medicine. This introduction to its available bounty informs those who want more certain nutritional benefits—and the pleasure of new and delicate sea tastes besides. From sea salt to wakame, from spirulina to the green-lipped mussel, there is much to learn for good health and good living.

ABOUT THE AUTHOR AND EDITORS

William H. Lee, R.Ph., Ph.D., has practiced pharmacy and has his doctorate in nutrition, in addition to a Master Herbalist's degree. He writes frequently for popular, professional and trade magazines on a variety of health-related subjects, and is a frequent lecturer at lay and professional meetings. He is a consultant to industry and to chiropractic and dental professional groups. Dr. Lee is the author of *The Book of Raw Fruit and Vegetable Juices and Drinks* and *Herbs and Herbal Medicine.*

Richard A. Passwater, Ph.D., is one of the most called-upon authorities for information relating to preventive health care. A noted biochemist, he is credited with popularizing the term "supernutrition" largely as a result of having written two bestsellers on the subject—*Supernutrition: Megavitamin Revolution* and *Supernutrition for Healthy Hearts.* His other books include *Easy No-Flab Diet, Cancer and Its Nutritional Therapies* and *Selenium as Food & Medicine.* He has just completed a new book, *Trace Elements, Hair Analysis and Nutrition* with Elmer M. Cranton, M.D.

Earl Mindell, R.Ph., Ph.D., combines the expertise and working experience of a pharmacist with extensive knowledge in most of the nutrition areas. His book *Earl Mindell's Vitamin Bible* is now a million-copy bestseller; and his more recent *Vitamin Bible for Your Kids* may very well duplicate his first *Bible's* publishing history. Dr. Mindell's popular *Quick & Easy Guide to Better Health* was published by Keats Publishing.

KELP, DULSE AND OTHER SEA SUPPLEMENTS

NUTRITIONAL TREASURES
THE OCEAN PROVIDES

by William H. Lee, R.Ph., Ph.D.

Keats Publishing, Inc. New Canaan, Connecticut

Kelp, Dulse and Other Sea Supplements is not intended as medical advice. Its intention is solely informational and educational. Please consult a medical or health professional should the need for one be warranted.

Contents

THE SEA WITHIN US

The source of all earthly life, including human beings, is the sea and all of the other bodies of water on the planet we call home. When we chose to leave our watery environment for life on land, we also chose to carry our native "soil" along with us. And, after millions of years, we continue to be dependent upon water.

Too much water can destroy us, but so can too little. The benefits of water on us, in us, and around us and the additional benefits of the vegetable and marine life that live in the sea are the focus of this booklet.

During our fetal period we go through certain stages of development that repeat our evolutionary beginnings. All of us show vestigial gill slits as we progress from egg to human form. All of us spend months of preparation for birth in an aqueous environment. When we enter the world of air, we carry the seas in our bloodstream.

Evolution has altered the composition of the sea from the time our first ancestors came ashore. Our blood probably more closely resembles the primeval concentrations, but the similarities remain very apparent.

An analysis of sea water today shows that it contains about 31 percent sodium, while human blood contains about 34 percent sodium. The concentrations of other elements, such as potassium, calcium, magnesium and chlorine are also overwhelmingly much the same in sea water and blood.

Next to oxygen, water is the most important factor for our survival. We can do without food for two months or even longer, but we can't do without drinking water for more than a few days. Although we drink pure water, not sea water, in certain circumstances a tablespoon of sea water daily can contribute to better health.

The oceans of the world make up about 70 percent of the earth's surface. They cover about 140 million square miles, with an estimated water volume of approximately 320 million cubic miles. That's an incredible area to be considered as a source of nutrients. There are vast oceans and forests waiting to be explored, tasted and utilized.

The primary life support system for all of mankind is the plant. Plants—from land or sea—are the basis of all life. In the sea, aquatic plants and plankton are the life-giving link. Plankton contains both plant (phytoplankton) and animal (zooplankton) groups. Phytoplankton, by utilizing sunlight and the nutritional treasures of the sea, synthesizes other foodstuffs in water. It begins the food chain for animal life. Many nations harvest both the fish and the vegetation that the seas provide, but such use is minimal in the United States. If you try to order seaweed in a conventional restaurant, you'll probably be turned out into the street. However, times are changing: seaweed is available in Japanese restaurants, and the dried variety is being sold in many markets.

There is no doubt that our vital needs are linked with the sea itself and with sea products. They can: relieve nutritional deficiencies; ease physical discomfort; help produce enzymes within the body itself; contribute to a longer life by helping to guard against small clots within the arteries; improve total health; replace essential minerals and trace minerals; and even provide food alternates to beef and chicken.

What is red, brown, green or blue-green, comes in 1700 varieties and waves gracefully from side to side? The answer is seaweed.

The main groups are classified according to their predominant color.

Brown seaweed. This group is usually found in cold waters, although a number of varieties are harvested in the warmer waters of the Pacific off the coast of California. Because they completely cover rocks between high and low tide, they are sometimes called rockweeds. The best known of the brown algae are the kelps. They generally grow in enormous beds just below the surface of the water. So fantastic is their growing ability, deriving nutrients only from the sun and surrounding water, that when they are harvested four feet from the surface, they grow back within ten days. Seaweeds do not have any roots. They cling to rocks with grippers, called holdfasts, which are strong enough to take the battering of even the fiercest storms.

Red seaweed. This grouping is usually a deep-water variety, up to 200 feet below the surface. Red seaweeds prefer shadier locations and warmer water than the brown variety. The color is probably because of the subdued light that barely reaches the deep waters. Irish moss is the best known of the red variety.

Green seaweed. This form of seaweed is closest to the green leafy vegetables with which we are familiar. In fact, one species is called sea lettuce. Green seaweed grows not only in the salty seas but also in fresh-water lakes and rivers. They are much smaller than the brown and red varieties, ranging in size down to the one-celled organism. Some green seaweed even grows on trees on land.

Seaweeds are used principally in human food, animal food, fertilizer and nutritional supplements. The nutritional supplement most readily found on health food store shelves is kelp. Kelp is a principal source of iodine, but that is only a part of the story.

Marine plants, such as the brown seaweed plant that is the source of kelp tablets and powder, live and flourish because of sunlight and the nutrients so plentiful in the sea.

In 1750, an English physician, Dr. Bernard Russell, burned dried kelp and used it successfully as a treatment for goiter, a condition caused by a malfunctioning of the thyroid gland. In 1862 a Dr. C. Dupare successfully used kelp as an aid to treat obesity. These uses depend on the iodine content, which kelp contains in natural form.

Iodine is said to benefit the body in other ways, in addition to promoting the proper functioning of the thyroid gland. It helps provide energy and endurance, and relieve nervous tension. Because iodine promotes circulation, particularly to the brain, it contributes to better nourishment and to clear thought. Iodine also helps to burn food, so it is not stored as unwanted fat.

Kelp contains almost every mineral and trace mineral necessary for human existence. It also contains amino acids and vitamins.

Everyone would do well to develop the habit of either taking kelp tablets every day, using kelp powder as a salt substitute (the iodine taste takes a little getting used to, but stick to it—the benefits are worth it!) or using the seaweed in salads. More about cooking with seaweed later.

There are a couple of other seaweed products you can find in health food stores. They are agar-agar and algin.

Agar-agar. Agar-agar is usually bought as a granular

powder. It can be used as a substitute for animal gelatin when making fruit jellies, aspics or molds. It is not as heavy or rigid as animal gelatin, but the results are highly satisfactory. Agar-agar is a rich source of vitamins, minerals and other trace elements as well as of iodine. Because it can add bulk to any meal without calories, agar-agar is helpful in curbing appetite when dieting.

Algin. Algin is a colloid found only in certain sea plants. It has the unique quality of being able to absorb large quantities of water. If one tablespoon of algin is dissolved in one quart of water, the mixture becomes so thick it can hardly be poured. This property has made it important to the ice cream and baking industries. However, it is in its role as an anti-pollutant that algin is most important. It is believed to be able to move through the body, drawing lead and other pollutants with it, so they can be eliminated from the body. Algin is usually found in tablet form, alone or combined with other nutrients.

Chemical Analysis of Kelp

	Percent		*Percent*
Protein	8.0	Carbohydrates	39
Fat	.3	Ash	35
Fiber	7.6	Moisture	10

Amino Acids

Lysine	Histidine
Methionine	Phenylalanine
Tryptophan	Cystine
Arginine	Leucine
Tyrosine	Isoleucine
Serine	Valine
Threonine	

Vitamins

Riboflavin   Choline
Niacin   Carotene

Minerals

Calcium   Zinc
Phosphorus   Sulphur
Iodine   Sodium
Iron   Sodium chloride
Copper   Potassium
Magnesium   Potassium chloride
Manganese
Many other trace elements

EDIBLE SEAWEEDS

Ninety-two different nutritional elements have been found in sea vegetation—including those trace elements whose presence, in tiny amounts, is vital to our wellbeing. An increasing number of nutritionists believe that every element found naturally in the earth's crust plays some role in human nutrition. Only lately has the trace mineral selenium been found to be vital to our life system. In the past, it was thought of only as a poison.

If it is conceded that all minerals are necessary to life, then the only way we can be sure of obtaining such rare minerals as natural boron, titanium, lithium, rubium and caesium is through products found in our seas.

Seaweeds contain many more minerals than do land plants. And our land mineral wealth is migrating slowly but steadily into the water. Unwise farming, wholesale mining and natural erosion are depleting the land of its mineral resources but enriching the sea. As our lands become poorer and the crops raised on those lands become more depleted of nutrients, the waters around us become a more vital source of food and medicine.

Although almost every country touched by the sea uses seaweed in one form or another, the Japanese are the largest users of seaweed as food. In Japan, seaweed is used as a condiment, vegetable, jelly, flavoring, soup stock base and salad.

The most commonly eaten species of seaweed are known as nori, kombu, wakame and hijiki. Nori is the most widely used. So important is this marine plant that its growth is not left to nature; it is cultivated as a regular crop in the Bay of Japan. Nori is gathered directly from the sea and used in soups and salads after a quick wash in clear water. It is also used as a breakfast dish with hot rice almost every morning in millions of Japanese homes. Nori can be dried into sheets and toasted. When a sheet of nori is filled with hot rice and either meat or fish, then rolled up, it is as convenient as any sandwich or hot dog. This delectable dish is known as sushi.

Kombu is derived from a number of seaweeds called laminaria, which like to live in the colder waters of the northern bay systems fed by the clear Arctic currents. Laminaria thrive in the icy depths. After harvesting, the plant is either dried or pre-cooked. Cooked kombu is a staple with rice, meat, poultry, fish or eggs. Dried kombu is usually used for soup stock and as a condiment. It can be powdered and put on the table to flavor various dishes in the same way we use salt or pepper. During holidays, squares of kombu are slowly dried until they are crisp. Then they are covered with a coating of sweet icing and used as candy. People who live near the shore gather and use the fresh seaweed, boiled to their taste, as a staple vegetable with a fish dinner.

Wakame, prepared from a large brown seaweed, can be used either dried or fresh. In its fresh form it is dipped in a rice vinegar sauce and enjoyed as a salad base. Dried, its main use is in the preparation of a soybean paste soup called miso. A product similar to our potato chips is made from dried wakame chips, and some people dip wakame in a sweet icing as a delicacy.

Hijiki is also a brown seaweed, which grows on rocks not too far from the shore line. It is generally used dried as a seasoning.

Kelp has been used as a rich source of natural iodine for centuries; however, there is a relatively unknown deep red seaweed that is one of the best natural sources of iron. It is called dulse, and in this hemisphere it is gathered by hand off the eastern coast of Canada from May until August. Besides having one of the highest concentrations of iron of any known food source, dulse is very rich in potassium for kidney function and magnesium for RNA and DNA production. Dulse also contains calcium. Although it is relatively unknown in the United States, some people, particularly in New England, use dulse as a healthful snack.

This seaweed may be the one to try first. You will be able to purchase it in its dried form in most health food stores. Try it first as a condiment or add small quantities to soup.

The amount of seaweed consumed at one given time is not large though it is considered a staple in the Japanese diet. It is mainly used as a flavor or relish, but the contribution it makes to health is enormous.

Although little seaweed is consumed in Europe and America, there is a long history pertaining to its use in the Northern Hemisphere. Sea lettuce and laminaria were eaten in England in the 1800s. Dulse has been boiled in milk to make pudding. Iceland has used dulse as a food for almost 2,000 years and even dried it for tobacco! Irish moss, cooked with milk and seasoned with fruit, is a nourishing dish, especially for those recovering from sickness.

Health food stores carry a number of dried seaweeds, which can be used the way the people who have used them for centuries add them to their table. Start with very small quantities and follow the directions printed on the package. If the taste is unusual at first, persist, because your body will welcome the nutritional benefits that follow.

FISH OIL FOR YOUR HEART'S SAKE

In several cultures around the world, fish have been the main source of dietary protein. Recent studies have indicated that certain circulatory and cardiac diseases are relatively rare among those who consume substantial quantities of fish, whale and seal. The possibility of a relationship between diet and disease has intrigued investigators for years. When they found that Eskimos began to suffer from vascular problems only after they left their villages and lived in the cities, researchers began to close in on the protective elements in the villagers' diets.

Because most of the fat in the traditional Eskimo diet comes from the oil of the fish they eat, it was surmised that the protective force must be in that type of oil. When that oil was examined they found a high concentration of an unusual fatty acid that was called Omega 3. This acid apparently originates in tiny algae and is passed up the natural food chain to larger fish which concentrate the fatty acid in their fat tissue. Omega 3 is chemically related to the land-based essential fatty acids called linoleic acid, linolenic acid and arachidonic acid.

A high concentration of Omega 3 was found in the blood of the Eskimos. It was suspected that this fatty acid could be the reason for their low incidence of clots, heart attack and stroke. Since a half-million people die each year because an artery that supplies blood to the heart has been suddenly blocked by a clot, the importance of this nutritional discovery is clear.

Omega 3 makes blood less viscous—less likely to clump

together. If the blood is more "slippery," there is less chance that it will form a clot within an artery. It will still clot where it's supposed to, but it's less likely to clot where it's not supposed to. Omega 3 can also help to lower blood cholesterol and triglyceride levels.

Prostaglandins, hormone-like substances manufactured in the body, regulate a very large number of cell activities. The body uses the oil that is available to it to manufacture these prostaglandins. If the available oil is from land plants, the prostaglandin is slightly different than if the available oil is from the sea. The body chooses the oil that is most abundant. PGH_2, manufactured from arachidonic or linoleic acid from vegetable oil, is not as favorable to the body as PGH_3, made from fish oil that contains the Omega 3. PGH_3 has protected the Eskimo, because it is that prostaglandin that gives the orders to make "slippery" blood.

The only reliable source of Omega 3 is fish oil. However, it is fish *body* oil that is needed and not fish *liver* oil. For example, the cod fish tends to concentrate its oil in the liver, while the mackerel stores its oil all over the body. Although cod liver oil contains Omega 3, you would have to take such an excessive amount to get enough of the Omega 3 that you would risk the danger of an overdose of vitamins A and D.

While it is advantageous to take cod liver oil daily in order to insure a good supply of vitamins A and D, it would also be a good idea to eat half a pound of mackerel every day in order to have a sufficient supply of Omega 3. Knowing the American diet however, it's not likely that this will happen. Omega 3 supplements are available, however; look for marine lipid concentrate (EPA-DHA) in supplement form. It is available in most health food stores.

SPIRULINA—A PLANETARY FOOD

Spirulina may be the superstar of the world's food supply. This tiny, blue-green algae is one of nature's original foods. It is high in protein, vitamins, minerals and essential fatty acids.

Spirulina can serve as a food source for a hungry world and as a supplement to a normal diet. It acts on the brain's appetite center to switch off hunger pangs while supplying deodorizing chlorophyll.

That's quite a lot to expect from an algae that's only one cell wide and about a millimeter in length. It is very light-sensitive and has the highest photosynthesis record of any known land or sea plant. Perhaps that's why it can develop such a storehouse of nutrients. It also serves to recycle carbon dioxide, replacing it with pure oxygen and thereby combatting pollution.

Spirulina grows in the world's oceans and on freshwater lakes. It is one of the basic links in the marine life food chain. We are not the first to use this remarkable little organism. Centuries ago the Aztecs in Mexico harvested the algae, dried it in the sun and used it as one of their food staples. The people of Chad and Niger harvest the algae from Lake Chad and sell green cakes in the market. Spirulina is easily produced, economical to market and highly nutritious.

The first marketers depended on the available nutrients in the lake and on the present environmental conditions. Now that spirulina has become a commercial crop as well as a nutritional supplement in the form of tablets, capsules or powder, it is cultivated in closed pond conditions with closely regulated sources of nutrients. It needs carbon dioxide and other nutrients for proper growth, and when they are supplied in abundance the growth rate is phenomenal. Spirulina can double its mass every few days.

Once it has been harvested, spirulina is homogenized and pasteurized. No chemicals are used for sterilization. Spirulina is a complete protein. That is, it can supply all twenty-one amino acids, including the *essential* amino acids (those we cannot manufacture in our bodies). Two tablespoons of the dried algae contain approximately thirteen grams of protein, more than most other natural foods. Even though spirulina is a plant, the cell walls are mostly protein (not cellulose, as in land plants) which means it is easily digestible. Spirulina can be compared to dried eggs, considered to be the most usable of all protein food. Eggs have an NPU (Net Protein Utilization) of 94 percent, because the essential amino acid portion of the egg is very close to that of the human body. Because the NPU of spirulina is very close to that of eggs, spirulina has been used in the treatment of protein-deficiency diseases.

Spirulina also contains the entire B-complex, although it is strongest in vitamins B1, B2, B3 and B12, with only traces of the rest of the B-complex family.

Spirulina's real strength lies in the fact that it is the strongest source of vitamin B12 ever to be found. Previously, it was thought that only animal tissue could provide much of this essential vitamin, although traces had been found in alfalfa and comfrey. But spirulina contains almost twice as much B12 as dried liver, which used to be considered the best source of the nutrient. Two tablespoons contain about thirty micrograms of vitamin B12, as compared to sixteen micrograms for the same amount of dried liver. And, spirulina tastes so much better.

Spirulina contains substantial amounts of beta-carotene, the substance the body converts to vitamin A. Beta-carotene recently caused a stir in the medical world, when it was revealed that it could help prevent lung cancer caused by smoking. Two tablespoons of spirulina contain about 9,000 International Units, or 180 percent of the recommended daily allowance.

Spirulina is rich in minerals, (including iron, phosphorus, zinc, potassium, magnesium, selenium and chromium. It is also a prime source of calcium, since it contains about twenty-six times the amount of calcium found in milk.

Spirulina can be used as a quick protein supply. Many athletes use it for an energy boost before sports. It is also ideal for backpackers as a source of nourishment. Spirulina's use as a dietary aid relates to its phenylalanine content. Phenylalanine is an amino acid that scientists believe can act on the appetite center of the brain to relieve hunger pangs. It has been used as an appetite suppressant.

Spirulina is available in most health food stores as a powder or as a tablet. If you use the powder and mix it with other foods, the result will be green in color—so be warned, and it won't surprise you!

HOPE FOR ARTHRITICS . . . FROM THE SEA

Sea water, with its natural nutrients and chemical balance so close to our blood supply, has often attracted man in hope of curing his ills. The air from the sea is pure and healthful, soothing mind and body. A sea voyage has often been recommended as a nerve tonic for the wealthy, while the less fortunate have had to settle for a trip to the beach. Sea-water baths were and are a traditional treatment for rheumatism.

Now, another therapy from the waters is being tried by thousands of people all over the world in the hope that it is the long-sought-after cure for arthritis. The unlikely source of this treatment is an extract derived from *Perna canaliculis*, the green-lipped mussel.

The arthritis treatment consists of daily doses of this extract, with most cases seeming to respond within a month.

Because the extract has been classified as a food and

not as a drug, it is usually found in health food stores and not in pharmacies. The companies producing the extract do not depend on mussels gathered by chance in the open sea. They are cultivated in giant marine farms and harvested during an eight-week period when the active ingredients are present in the mussel. This permits a controlled environment with freedom from pollution.

One problem is the possibility of allergy. If a person is allergic to seafood, it is very likely he will also be allergic to the extract. Patients who are allergic have reported skin rashes and dizziness. Other minor side effects have been reported, although they are rare.

Although the active ingredient in the extract is still now known, the following substances have been identified:

alanine	manganese
arginine	methionine
aspartic acid	nickel
calcium	phenylalanine
carbohydrates	potassium
copper	proline
cysteic acid	protein
cystine	selenium
fats	serine
glutamic acid	sodium
glycine	threonine
histidine	tyrosine
iron	valine
iso-leucine	vitamin A
lysine	vitamin B complex
magnesium	zinc

Even the manufacturers do not claim that the extract is a cure for arthritis, but there seems to be some basis for recommending a trial. The extract possesses an exceptional degree of biological activity that is unique. It is rare to find such a balanced mixture of nutrients. Eggs exemplify that balance, representing nutrients in an embryonic state but not in a functional body cell state. When we cook the egg, we destroy most of the potentially useful material.

One of the mysteries that led scientists to study the *Perna canaliculus* mussel was that the mussel does not age and die as most humans do. It remains in a youthful state for seventy to eighty years or longer, and dies only because its nutrient needs become greater than the environment can supply.

In addition, the mussel never shows signs of any type of malignancy. Thousands of them have been examined, and tissue biopsies confirm their freedom from malignant disease.

SEA SALT, SEA SUGAR, SEA STARCH

Sea water is salty, but it contains much more than sodium chloride (the common salt we have on our tables). It is composed of sodium and chlorine (which makes up sodium chloride) plus magnesium, calcium, potassium, sulfates, strontium, bromine, boron, carbon, hydrogen, oxygen and at least thirty-six more chemical elements and minerals.

However, sea water also contains dissolved vitamins, enzymes, amino acids and other nutrients. When we swim in sea water, we bathe our bodies in all of those healthful ingredients.

Islanders, such as the Melanesians, dip their food into sea water as if it were a condiment. You can sip a bit of sea water daily if you don't exceed your daily salt ration. Sipping sea water can normalize your stomach acid content. If you have too much acid, sea water will reduce it. If you have too little acid, sea water will increase it!

Throw away your common table salt and buy sea salt instead. It will serve the same purpose as regular table salt and give you needed minerals as well. It can also act as a curative for a number of ills. Folklore says sea salt works without the side effects caused by certain drugstore remedies or doctor's prescriptions.

REMEDIES FOR COMMON ILLS

Head cold. Get an infant-sized rubber syringe. It looks like a rubber ball with a nozzle and is sold in every drugstore. Mix one teaspoon of sea salt with four ounces of milk and eight ounces of warm water. Fill the rubber syringe with the mixture and squirt it gently into your nose. The mixture will run into your throat, and then you will be able to spit it out. This treatment sounds crude, but it is said to provide almost immediate relief from head colds.

Sore throat. Put two teaspoons of sea salt into eight ounces of warm water and gargle.

Toothache. If a cavity is the cause, mix a bit of alum (available from the drugstore) and a bit of sea salt. Moisten a dab of cotton with warm water and dip it into the mixture. Pack the cavity with the cotton and see your dentist as soon as possible.

Heartburn. Dissolve a tiny amount of sea salt in your mouth. It should relieve the heartburn at once.

Eyewash. Boil and cool some water. Add a tiny pinch of sea salt to two tablespoons of water. Bathe the eyes in the mixture.

Itching. Add two ounces of sea salt to your bath water and soak for fifteen minutes.

General tonic. Sip a little bit of sea water every day.

If you use salt, it's a good idea to have a banana every day so that there is a balance of minerals. Alternate sea salt with powdered kelp, using one every other day, or use powdered dulse. You will be very pleasantly surprised at the different taste sensations you get from using different condiments on the same dish. The flavor of eggs, for example, will be changed in a way you'll never get tired of.

If ordinary sugars from land plants do not agree with you, then perhaps the marine equivalent of those sugars will. They are called mannitol and are found in the young stalks of sugar wrack or tang.

Likewise, if the ordinary land starches do not agree with your system, then the marine version may. It's called laminaria and is derived from a kelp.

Although mannitol and laminaria are not easily found, even in health food stores, you might ask your local store to place a special order for them.

COOKING WITH SEA VEGETABLES

Here are a few sea vegetable recipes you can try. Then, when you find you like the results, you may want to buy a cookbook on the subject.

Carrot soup flavored with wakame

> 1 *cup soaked wakame* (wash the wakame in cold running water, then let it soak for ten minutes)
> 2 *celery stalks*
> 1 *onion, sliced*
> 2 *medium-sized carrots, diced*
> 4 *cups of water*
> 2 *teaspoons Tamari soy sauce*

Cut the wakame into small squares. Put all of the ingredients into a pot, bring to a boil, then let simmer for ten minutes. Remove from heat. Stir. Add tamari and serve. Serves two.

Japanese bean soup

First make a stock called dashi:

> 1 *sheet nori*
> 4 *cups water*
> ½ *cup dried bonito flakes*

Place the nori in water and bring to a boil. Simmer for five minutes. Add the bonito flakes and turn off the heat. Let stand until the flakes sink to the bottom. Then strain. The broth remaining is dashi.

Use:

> 2½ cups dashi
> 3 tablespoons soybean paste (miso)
> 3 cubes of tofu (bean curd)

Combine the dashi and the soybean paste. Stir until dissolved. Heat without boiling, and add the tofu. For added flavor and nutrition slice in mushrooms, water chestnuts and green onions. Heat thoroughly and serve.

Seaweed salad

> 1 pound fresh Irish moss
> ¼ cup rice vinegar
> ½ tablespoon crushed fresh ginger
> ½ green onion, chopped
> sea salt to taste

Soak the seaweed in boiling water until transparent (a few minutes). Rinse in cold water. Drain. Mix all ingredients in a salad bowl and toss. Chill for one hour before serving.

Ice cream from the sea

Here's a recipe you will be proud of. Nobody has to know how you made it until after they've tasted it.

> ½ cup agar-agar
> 1 egg white
> ½ cup cream
> 1 ounce honey
> 2 cups water
> ¼ teaspoon vanilla

Cover the agar-agar with water and steep until soft (15 minutes). Add other ingredients. Stir and heat gently to just under the boiling point. Simmer 15 to 20 minutes. Pour into a mold and chill thoroughly. Serve.

Although these dishes may seem strange at first (serve them in small portions until your family and friends get used to the taste), they are so nutritious and their mineral content so varied that they should become part of your diet.

SEA SOURCES OF VITAMINS, MINERALS AND ENZYMES

We are told that the best way to keep healthy is to insure a continuous supply of all the necessary nutrients. Your body requires proteins, fats and oils, carbohydrates, minerals and vitamins. However, land plants and animals are becoming increasingly deficient in certain nutrients.

You need a broad and varied diet that includes seafoods. Seafood can be a particularly good source of protein, which builds and repairs body tissue, fights infection, provides energy and makes hemoglobin (the oxygen-carrying element in blood). Protein is broken down in the digestive tract into amino acids and then rebuilt into the proteins the body needs.

The following Table favorably compares the percentages of the essential amino acids in fish and in beef:

	Percentage in 3 ounces of fish	3 ounces of beef
Lysine	9.0	8.0
Leucine	7.0	7.0
Valine	5.8	5.8
Phenylalanine	4.5	4.9
Isoleucine	6.0	6.3
Threonine	4.5	4.6
Methionine	3.5	3.3
Histidine	2.4	2.9
Tryptophan	1.3	1.9
Arginine	7.4	7.7

Marine algae also contain protein—not in the quantity found in fish, but more than in beans and peas.

Fats and oils are abundant in seafood, as are healthful amounts of necessary cholesterol. Along with the cholesterol is the protective fish oil.

Carbohydrates are found in seaweed if they are found at all. Fish contain about 1 percent carbohydrates; clams, however, contain more than 4 percent. But don't put clams down! Some doctors recommend oysters and clams for diabetics on a restricted diet. First, eating oysters and clams is a joy, not a chore. Second, they're bulky and a full meal can be made from six or eight of them. Third, they make a balanced meal. Fourth, shellfish contain copper and zinc. Copper is said to help insulin act over a longer period of time, while zinc activates the available insulin.

And now to vitamins and minerals. Take a vitamin/mineral tablet every day. As often as you can, eat six ounces of a fatty fish. Six ounces will provide you with:

- two and a half times the RDA of vitamin D
- all of your vitamin A needs
- three-quarters of the RDA for niacin
- half of your daily protein
- half of your daily fat
- and a good part of your RDA for phosphorus, iron, and vitamins B1 and B2.

Dr. Benjamin Frank in his book *The No Aging Diet* recommends that people eat a can of sardines every day. Sardines are a natural source of RNA and DNA, the nucleic acids, and he says the patients who follow his advice look and feel younger.

RNA (ribonucleic acid) and DNA (deoxyribonucleic acid) dictate everything that happens in the cell. DNA in the nucleus gives the orders, and RNA on the periphery carries them out. The quality of the nucleic acids deteriorates as we grow older, and faulty cells are created. They, in turn, create more faulty cells and speed up the degenerative process.

According to Dr. Frank, RNA and DNA from outside sources can contribute substantially to the process of returning those cells to a healthy state. That means increased youth and delayed old age.

The nucleic acid content of the following foods can serve as a guide:

Fresh Seafoods

Sardines	343 mg
Anchovies	341 mg
Salmon	289 mg
Mackerel	203 mg
Squid	100 mg
Clams	85 mg

Canned Seafoods

Sardines	590 mg
Oysters	239 mg
Mackerel	122 mg
Herring	82 mg
Clams	44 mg
Salmon	26 mg
Shrimp	10 mg
Anchovies	6 mg
Tuna	5 mg

One of the side benefits of eating canned sardines seems to be a significantly lowered cholesterol.

HELP YOURSELF TO HEALTH

Sea nutrients are invaluable for energy and reconstruction of the body. Even if you don't live near the sea, you can "fish" on the shelves of your health food store for kelp tablets or powder, various dried seaweeds, agar-agar, sea salt, EPA-DHA or MaxEPA, spirulina and sea water.

If you want fish that's low in fat and high in protein, choose from cod, flounder, haddock, hake, mullet, perch, pollack, rockfish or whiting. Scallops and shrimp are also low fat-high protein.

High fat-high protein fish are mackerel, anchovies, herring, salmon and sardines. All other fish are between these two groups in fat content.

If you live near a beach and cultivate a garden, bring home as much of the seaweed as you can find and use it as fertilizer for your plants. Don't throw away the parts of the fish you don't cook. Bury them at the feet of your plants, and watch them bloom.

Bathe as often in the sea as you can. When you can't bathe, breathe deeply of the fresh sea air.

The sea was our mother, and she still cares for her children.

- **Kelp, Dulse and Other Sea Supplements** by William H. Lee, R.Ph., Ph.D.
- **Lysine, Tryptophan and Other Amino Acids** by Robert Garrison, Jr., R.Ph., M.A.
- **Nutrition and Exercise for the Over 50s** by Susan Smith Jones, Ph.D.
- **Nutrition and Stress** by Harold Rosenberg, M.D.
- **A Nutritional Guide for the Problem Drinker** by Ruth Guenther, Ph.D.
- **Nutritional Parenting** by Sara Sloan
- **Octacosanol, Carnitine and Other "Accessory" Nutrients Vol. 2** by Jeffrey Bland, Ph.D.
- **The Orotates** by William H. Lee, R.Ph., Ph.D.
- **Propolis: Nature's Energizer** by Carlson Wade
- **Spirulina** by Jack Joseph Challem
- **A Stress Test for Children** by Jerome Vogel, M.D.
- **Tofu, Tempeh, Miso and Other Soyfoods** by Richard Leviton
- **Vitamin B3 (Niacin)** by Abram Hoffer, M.D., Ph.D.
- **Vitamin C Updated** by Jack Joseph Challem
- **Vitamin E Updated** by Len Mervyn, Ph.D.
- **The Vitamin Robbers** by Earl Mindell, R.Ph., Ph.D.
- **Wheat, Millet and Other Grains** by Beatrice Trum Hunter